# Hello!

My name is Jade Elizabeth (Color Me Forum™) and I am the artist behind these pages! Thank you so much for purchasing them, your support means so much to me!

I hope you love this book, whether you love mandalas or maybe not, and find these new perspectives both refreshing and inspiring! This book should be great for travelling with, using in waiting rooms, and portable enough to go anywhere you can go…so I hope you love it and it rescues you from boredom and stress everywhere you travel to!

I'd love to hear from you so feel free to write me back!

Happy Coloring!
Jade Elizabeth (Color Me Forum™)


# P.S. Join Me!

If you'd like to join other coloring enthusiasts like yourself you're welcome to join us free on ColorMeForum.com/f (our forum).

Our happy forum is dedicated to sharing knowledge, experiences, and most of all our love of coloring. I can't wait to see you there!

You can also find me by searching Color Me Forum™ on Facebook, Instagram, Pinterest, Twitter, G+ and Youtube. If you'd like to support me further, and be rewarded for it, please consider supporting me via Patreon at patreon.com/ColorMeForum. Thanks again! <3

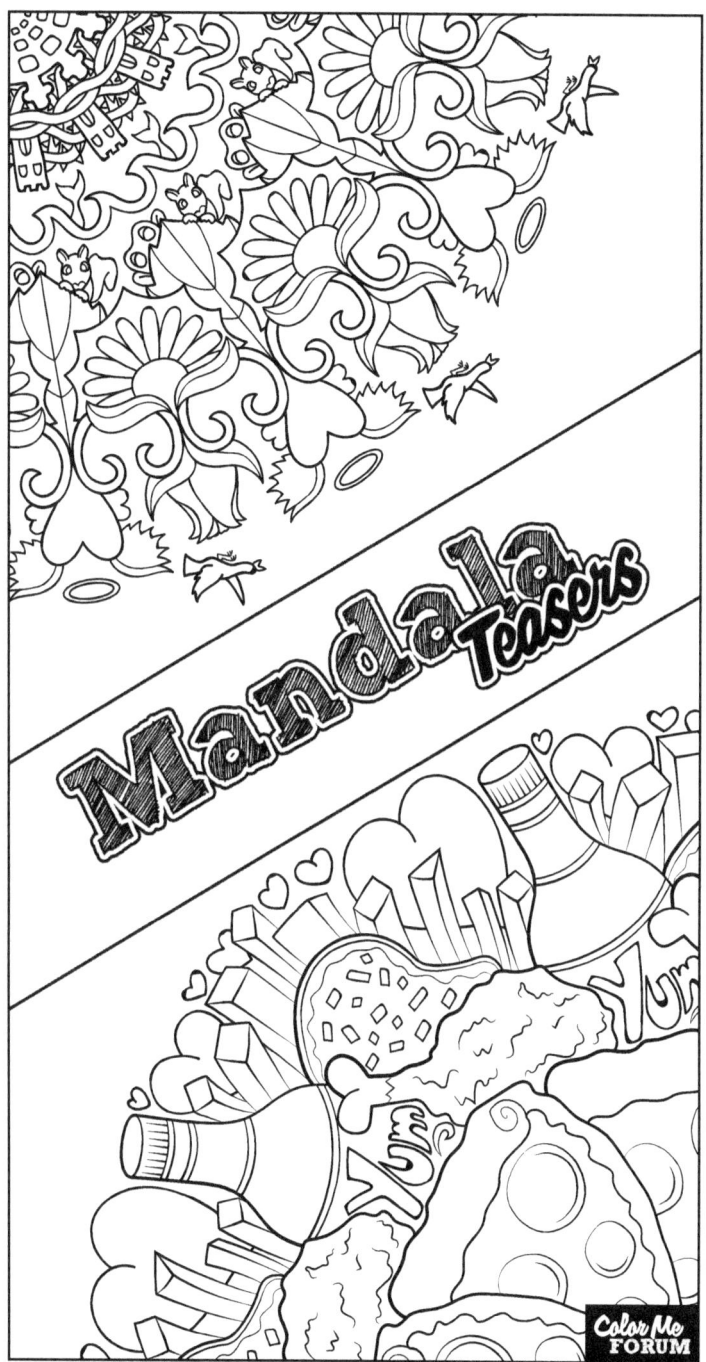

## A Note About Copyright…

I know it's an icky topic no one wants to talk about, but accidental piracy hurts budding and established artists more than you could ever imagine! We work hard for your enjoyment, it can take days to make a single page…so please consider the following…

1. You may not make copies of the pages/linework in this book for friends, family, commercial use, derivative works, or to give away. Each person must purchase their own book.

2. You may not take pictures of the pages while blank (uncolored) to give away, sell, or share online.

3. You must leave my logo intact & visible when sharing the colored in page online and credit me as the artist.

***Thanks so much for your understanding! Happy Coloring!***

**Color Me Forum™ Mandala Teasers Volume 1**

© 2017 by Color Me Forum™. All rights reserved.

No part of this publication may be reproduced, modified, altered, distributed, or transmitted in any form or by any means, including photocopying, recording, or other electronic or mechanical methods, without the prior written permission of the author and artist, Color Me Forum™, except in the case of brief quotations embodied in critical reviews and certain other noncommercial uses permitted by copyright law. Contact the author and artist, Jade Elizabeth, via email: admin@colormeforum.com.

ISBN-13: 978-1977721419
ISBN-10: 1977721419
Volume 1
Find more pages at www.ColorMeForum.com/store

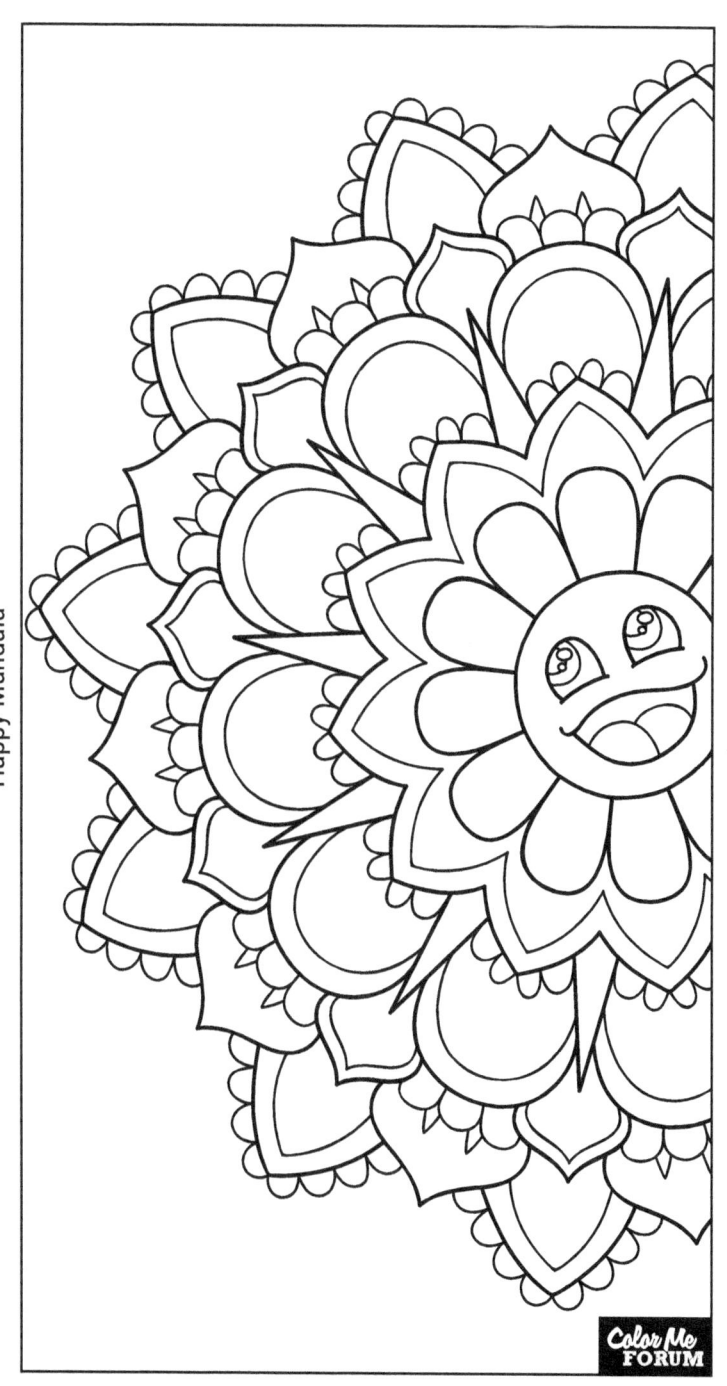

Mandala Teasers by Color Me Forum™

Mandala Mandala

Mandala Teasers by Color Me Forum™

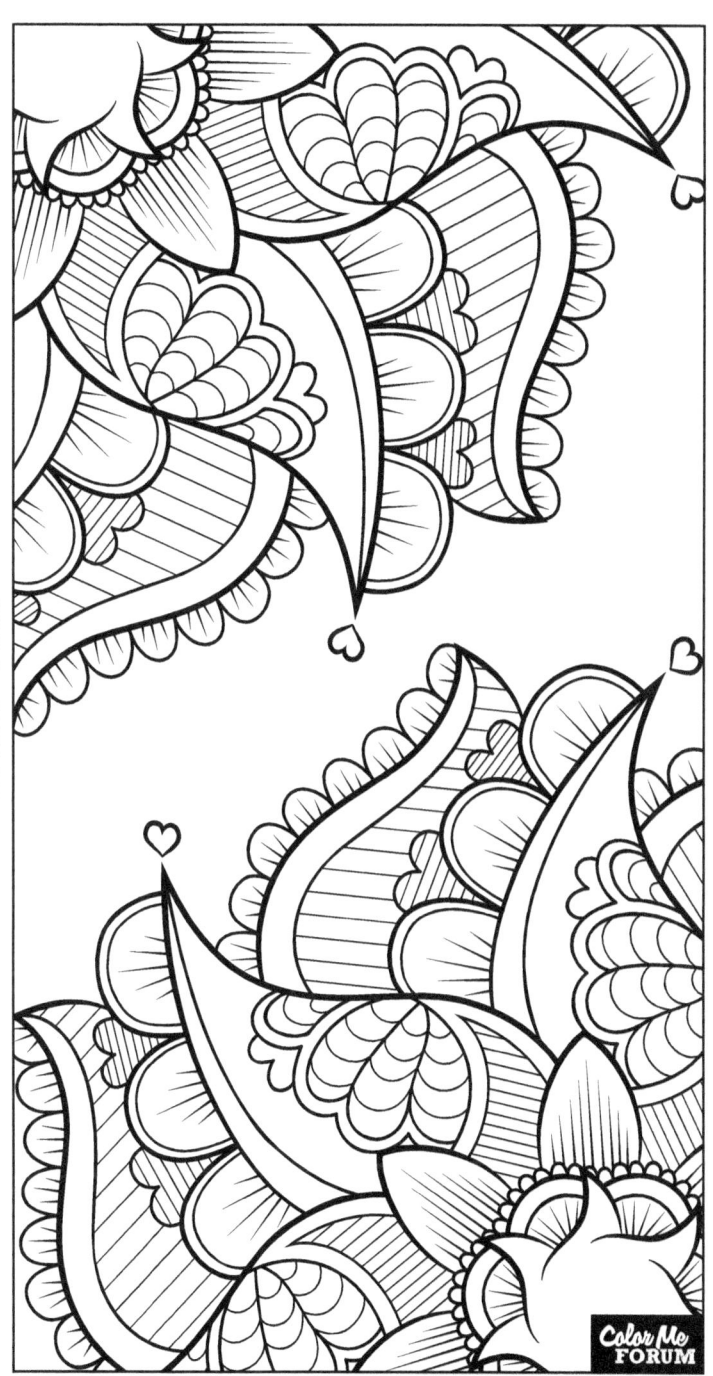

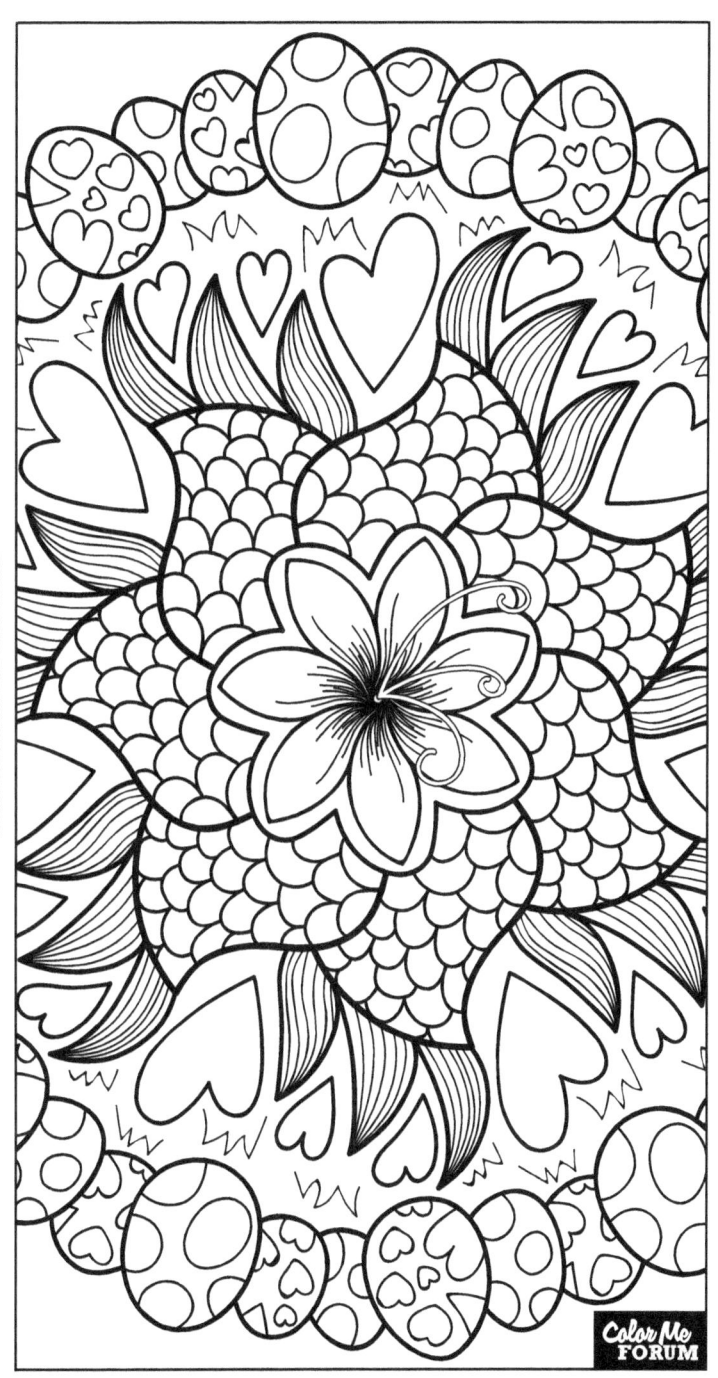

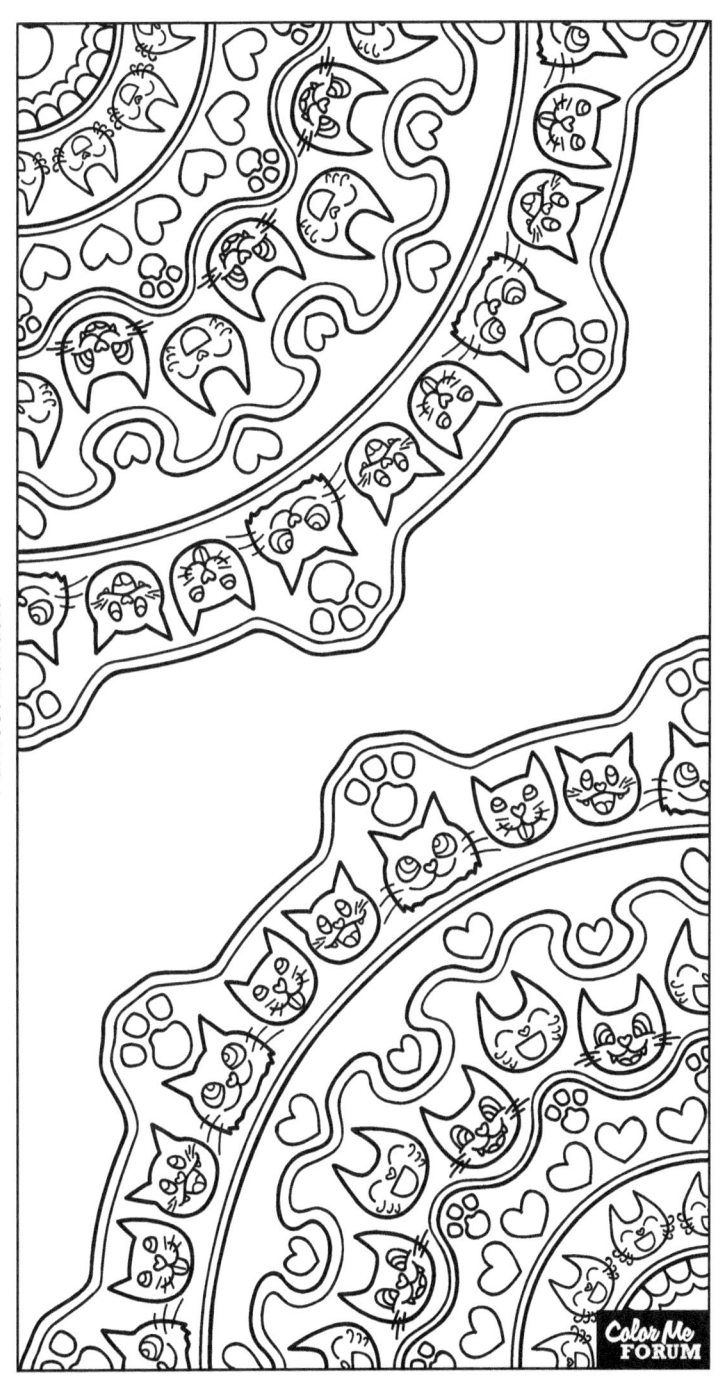

Bee Garden Mandala

Mandala Teasers by Color Me Forum™

Pizza Party Mandala

Mandala Teasers by Color Me Forum™

Birdies Mandala

Mandala Teasers by Color Me Forum™

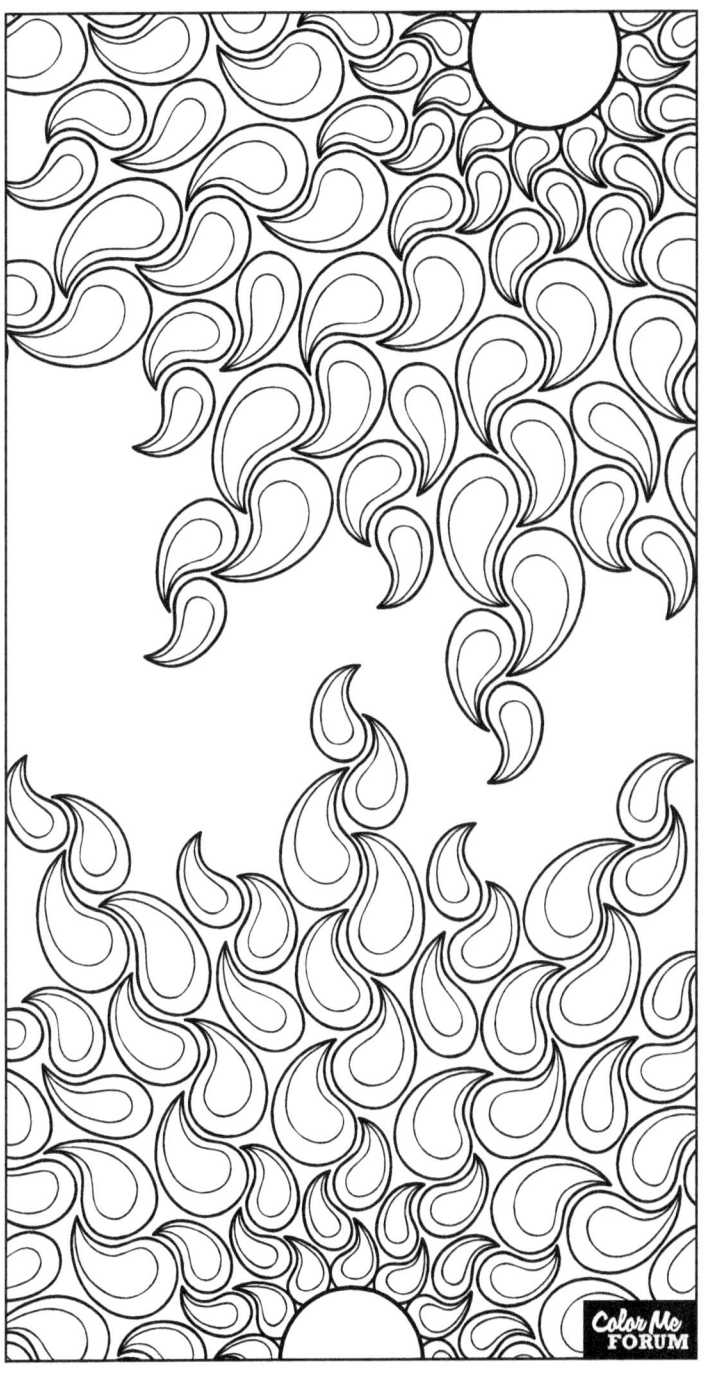

Star Spiral Mandala

Mandala Teasers by Color Me Forum™

Firecracker Mandala

Mandala Teasers by Color Me Forum™

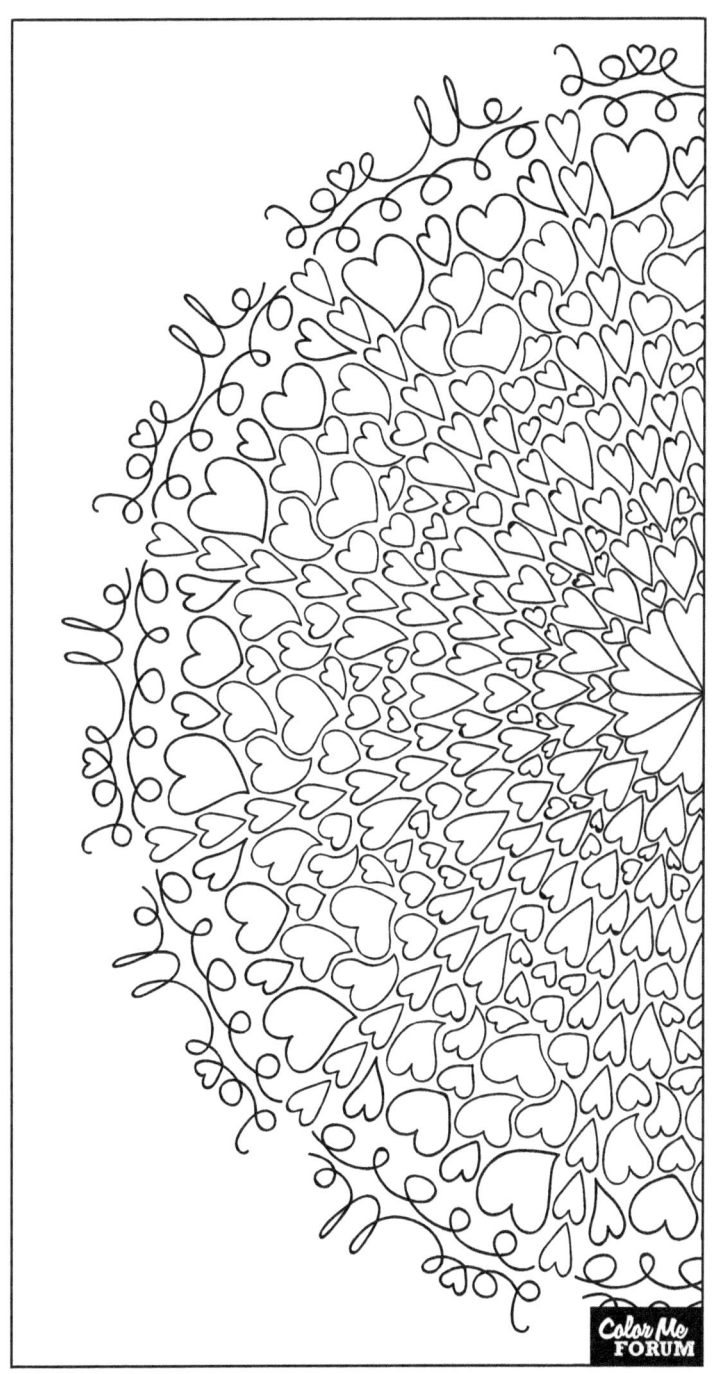

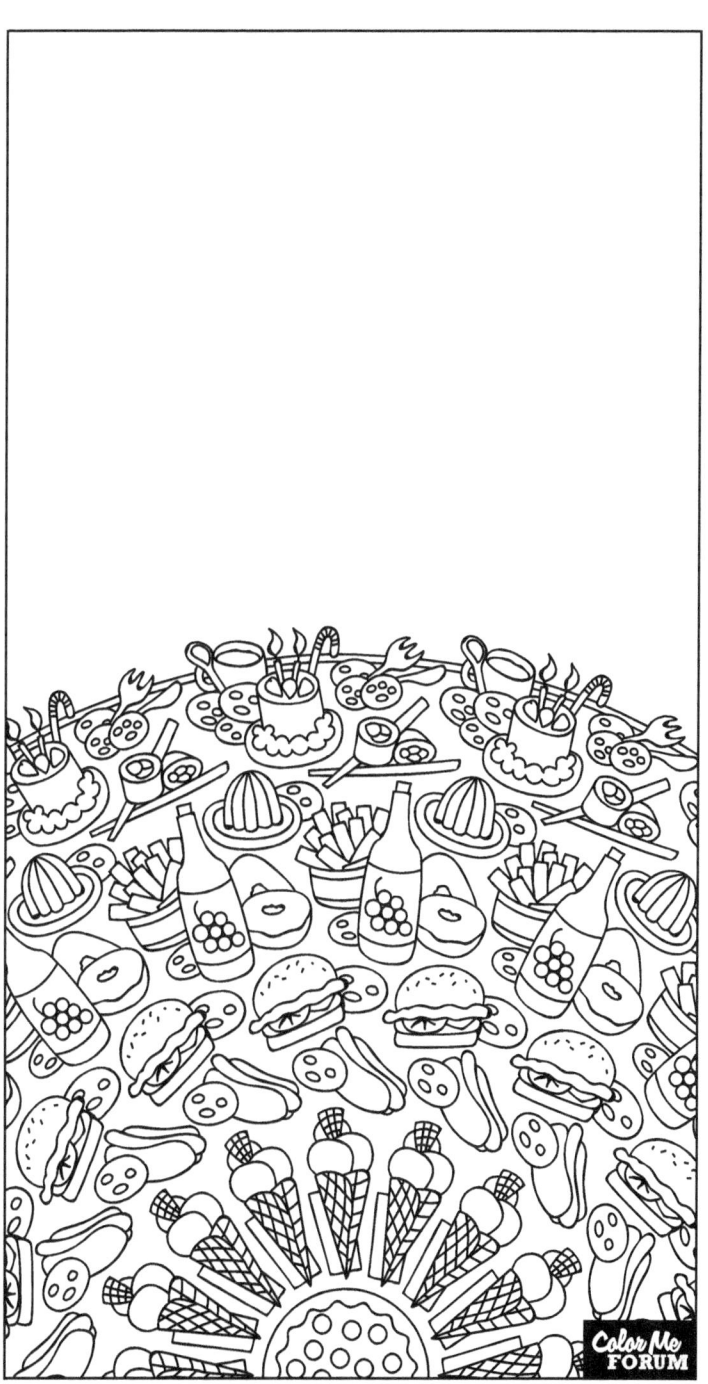

Little Daisy Mandala

Mandala Teasers by Color Me Forum™

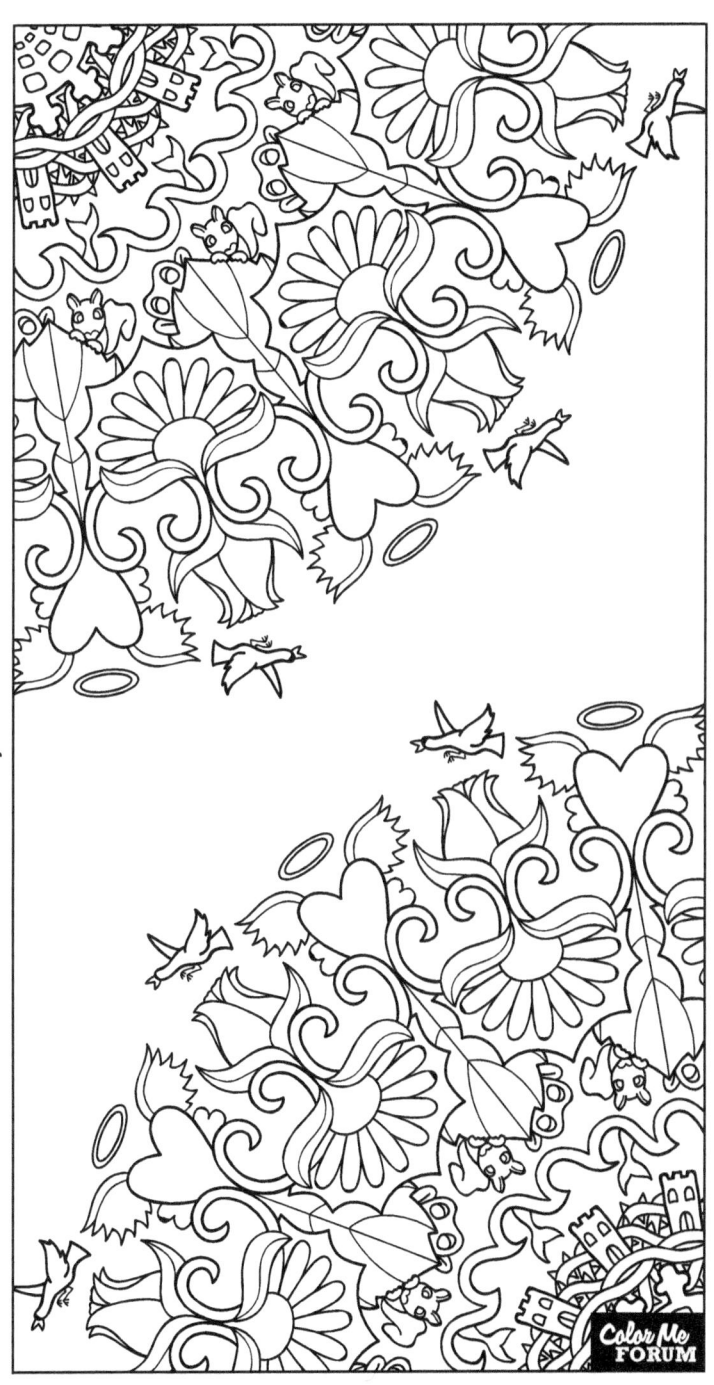

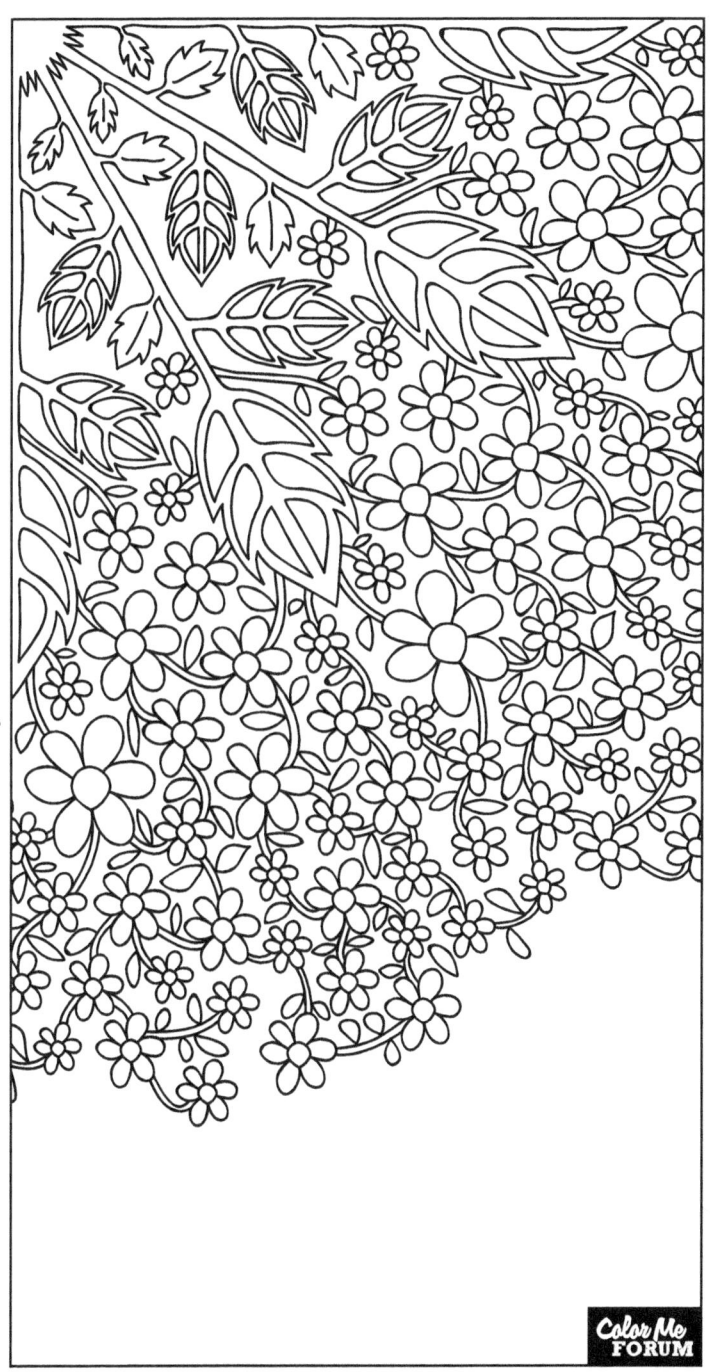

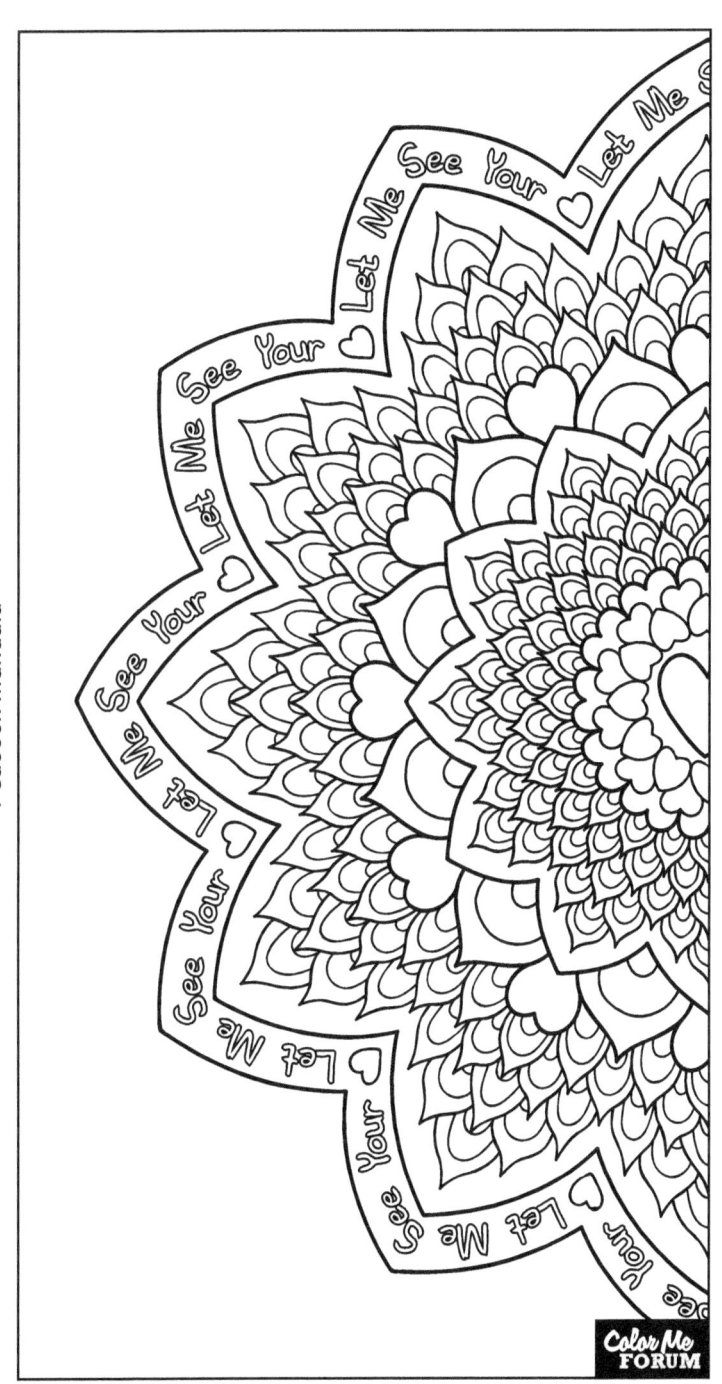

Peacock Mandala

Mandala Teasers by Color Me Forum™

Mandy Mandala

Mandala Teasers by Color Me Forum™

Kitties Mandala

Mandala Teasers by Color Me Forum™

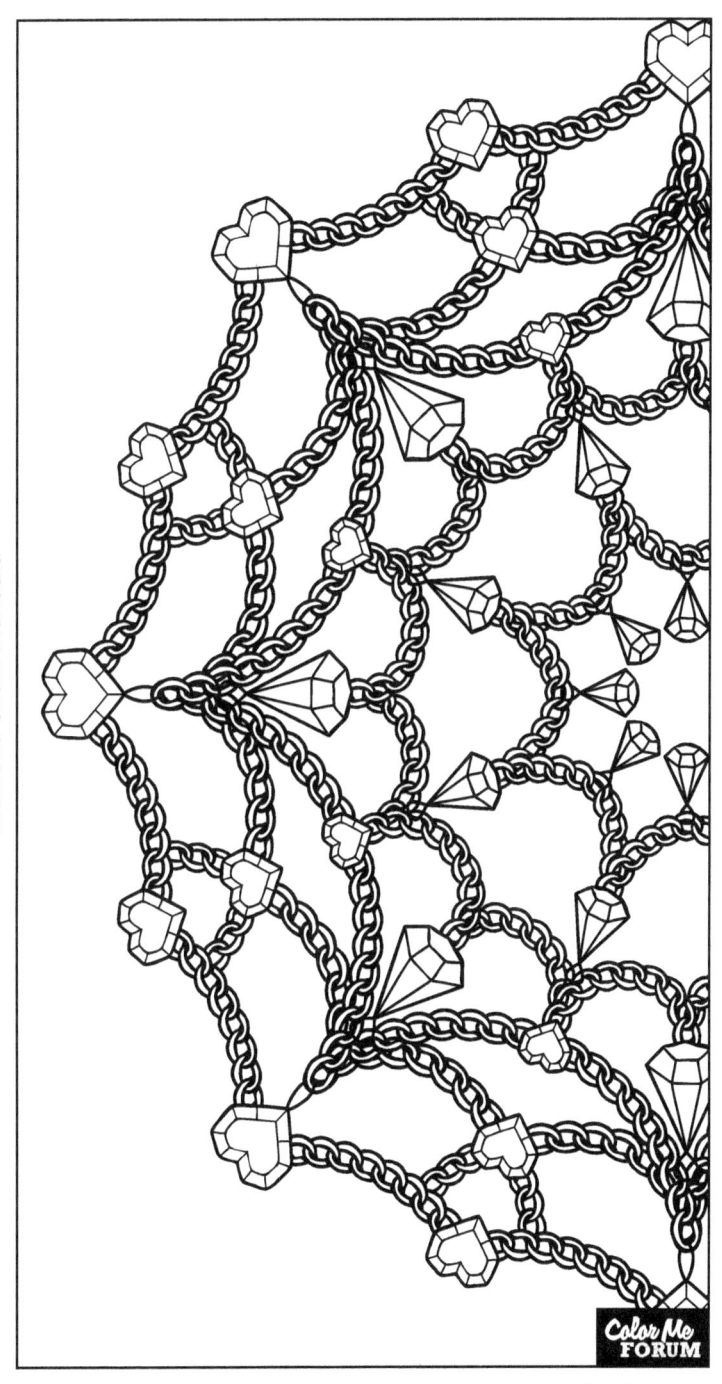

Mandala Mandala

Mandala Teasers by Color Me Forum™

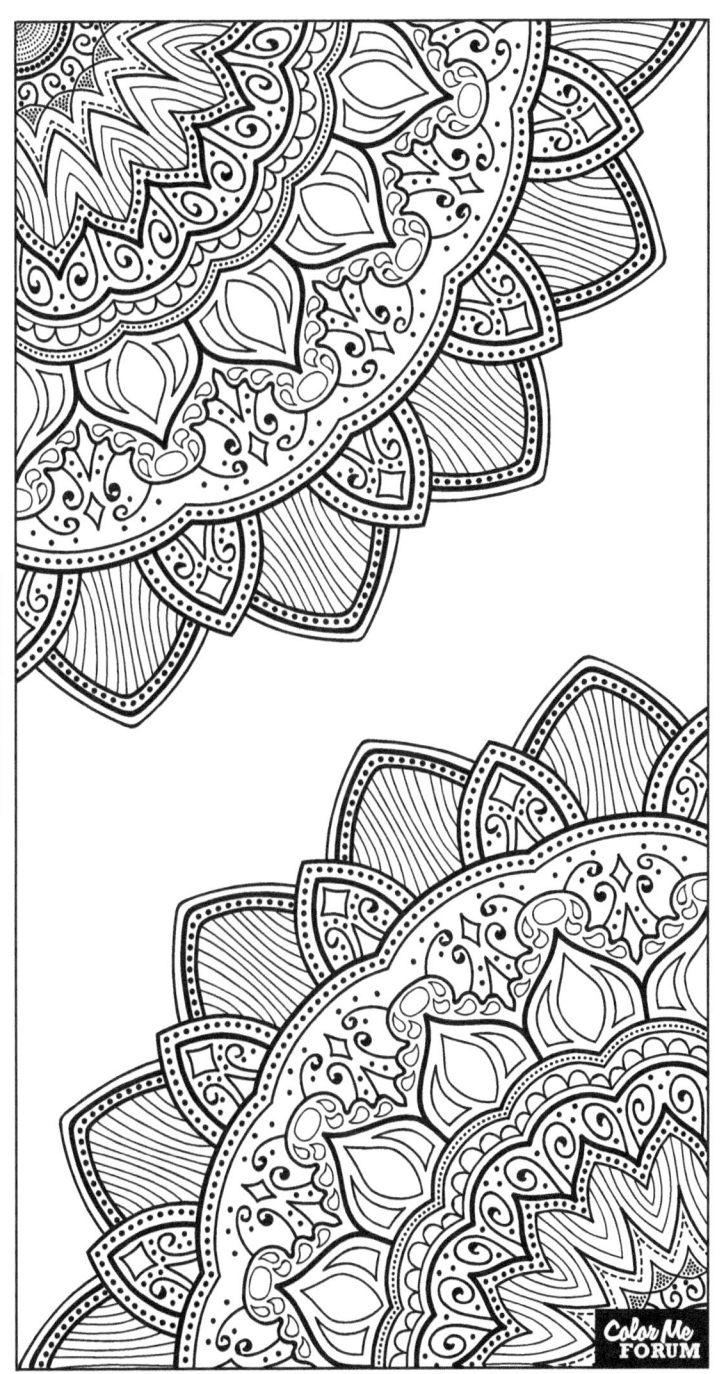

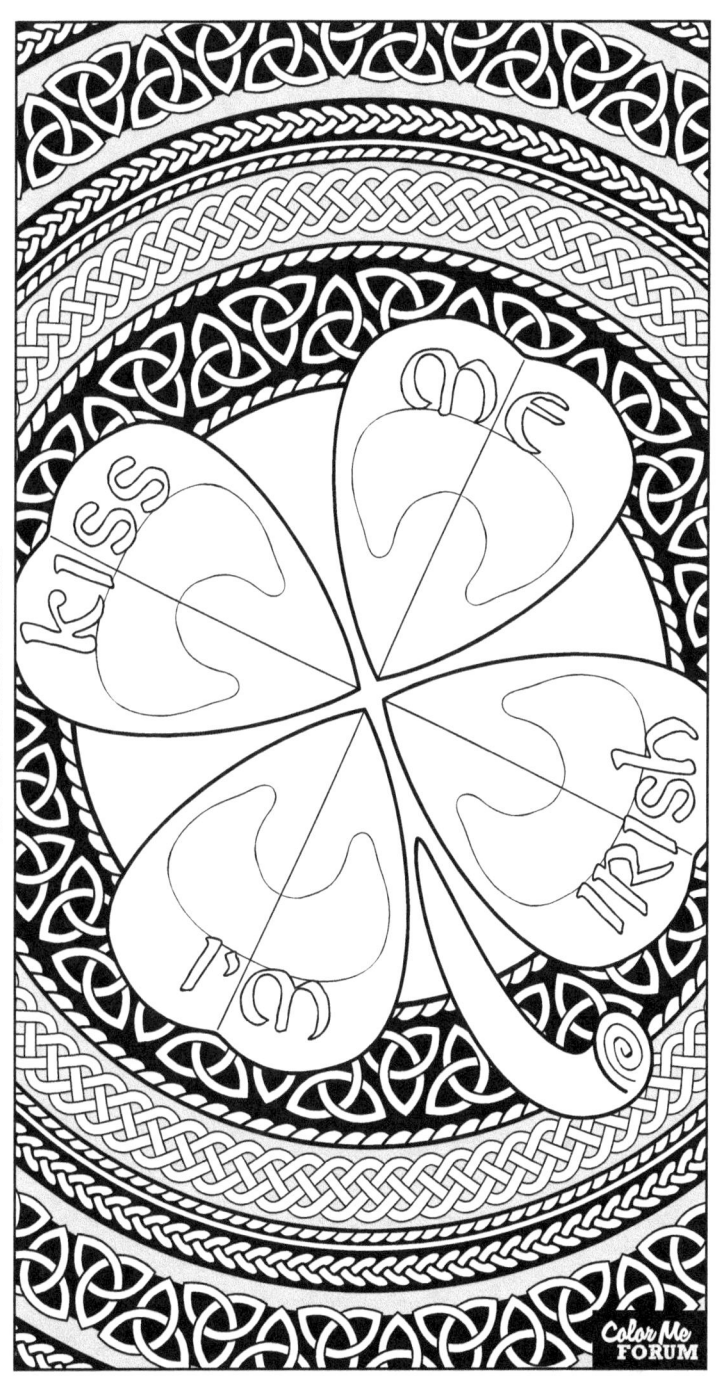

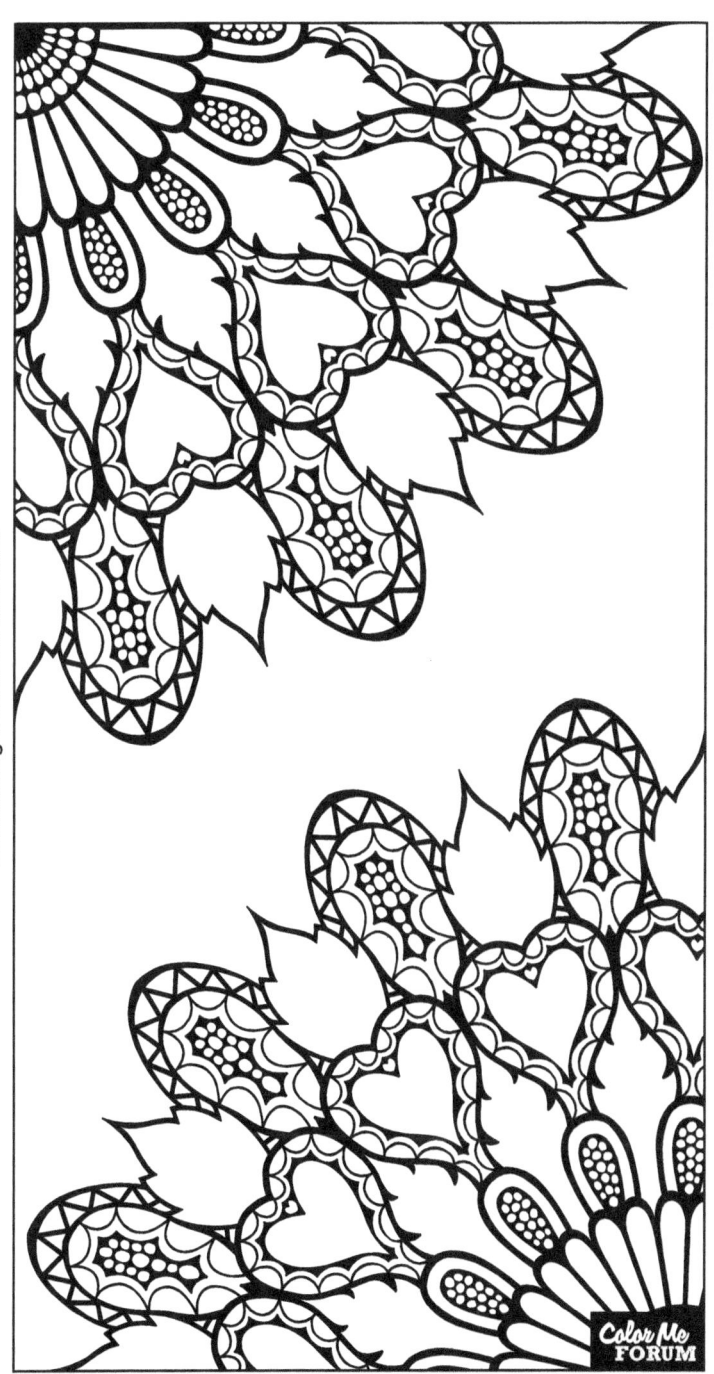

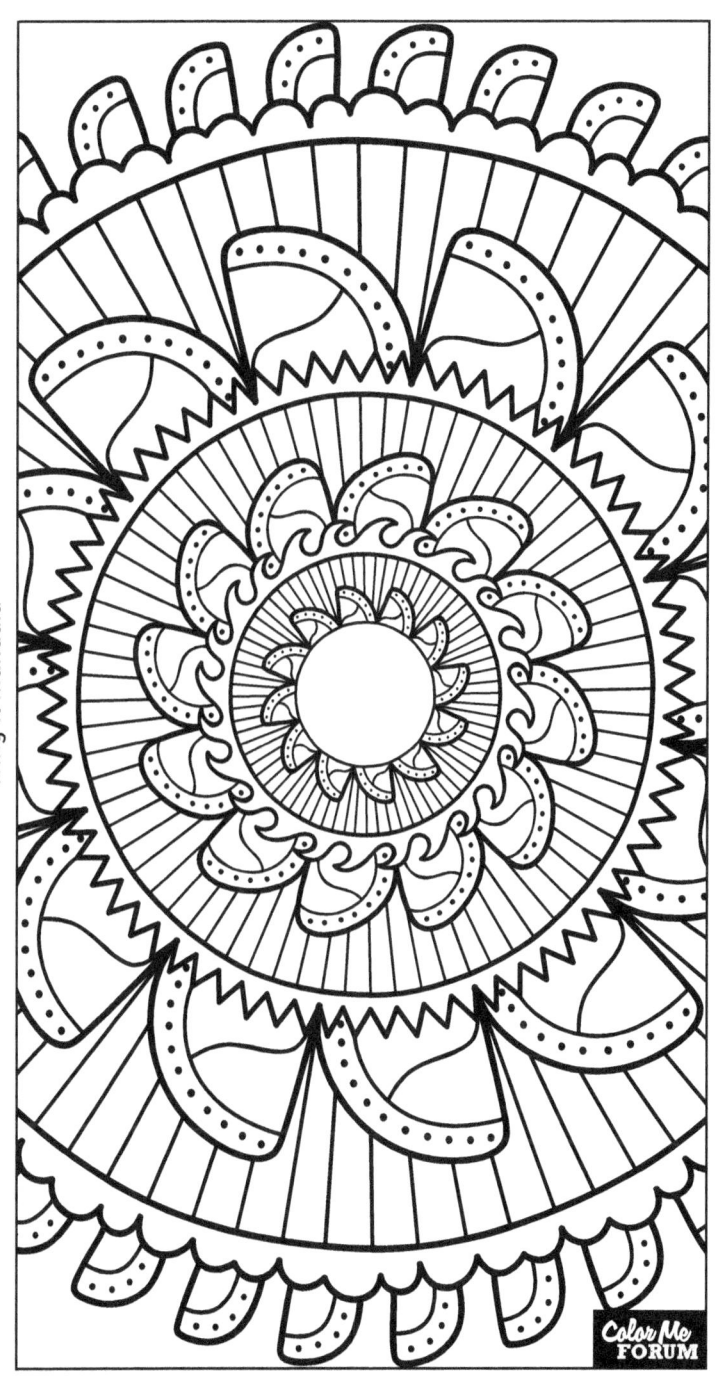

Mandala Teasers by Color Me Forum™

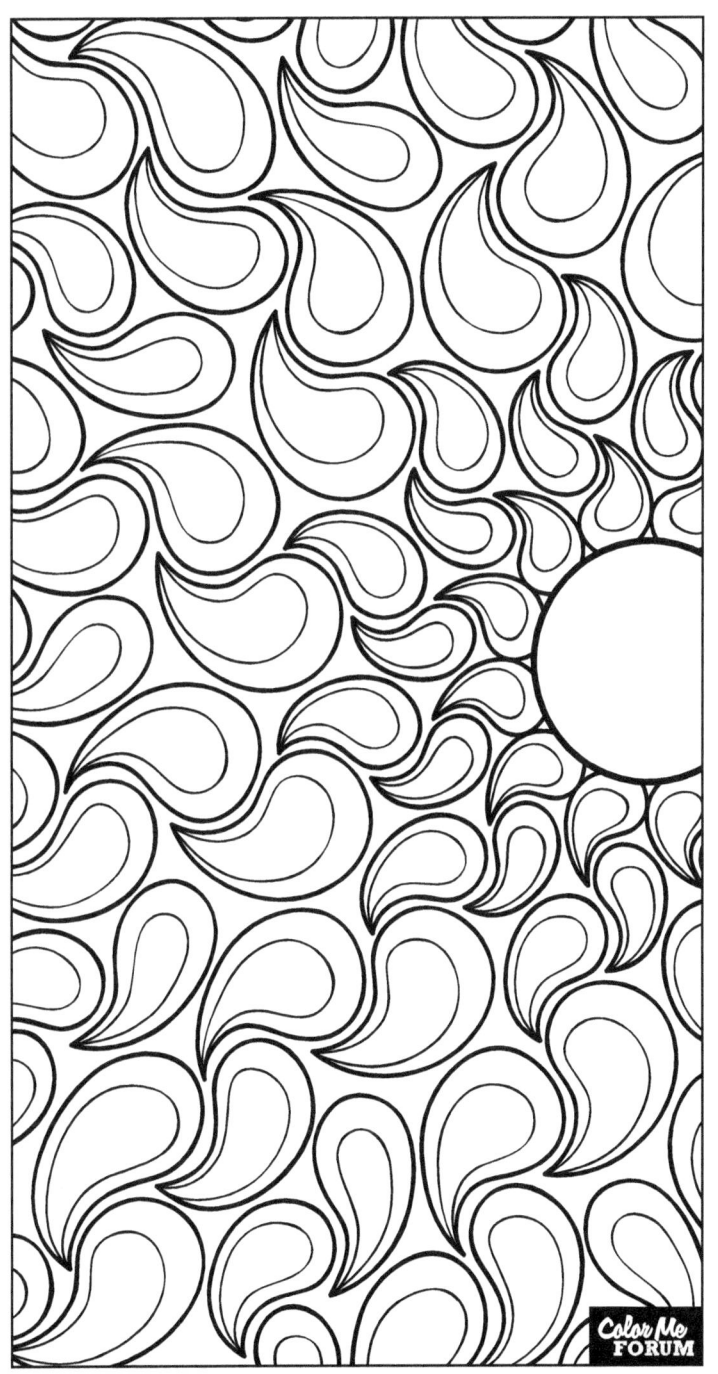

Foodie Mandala

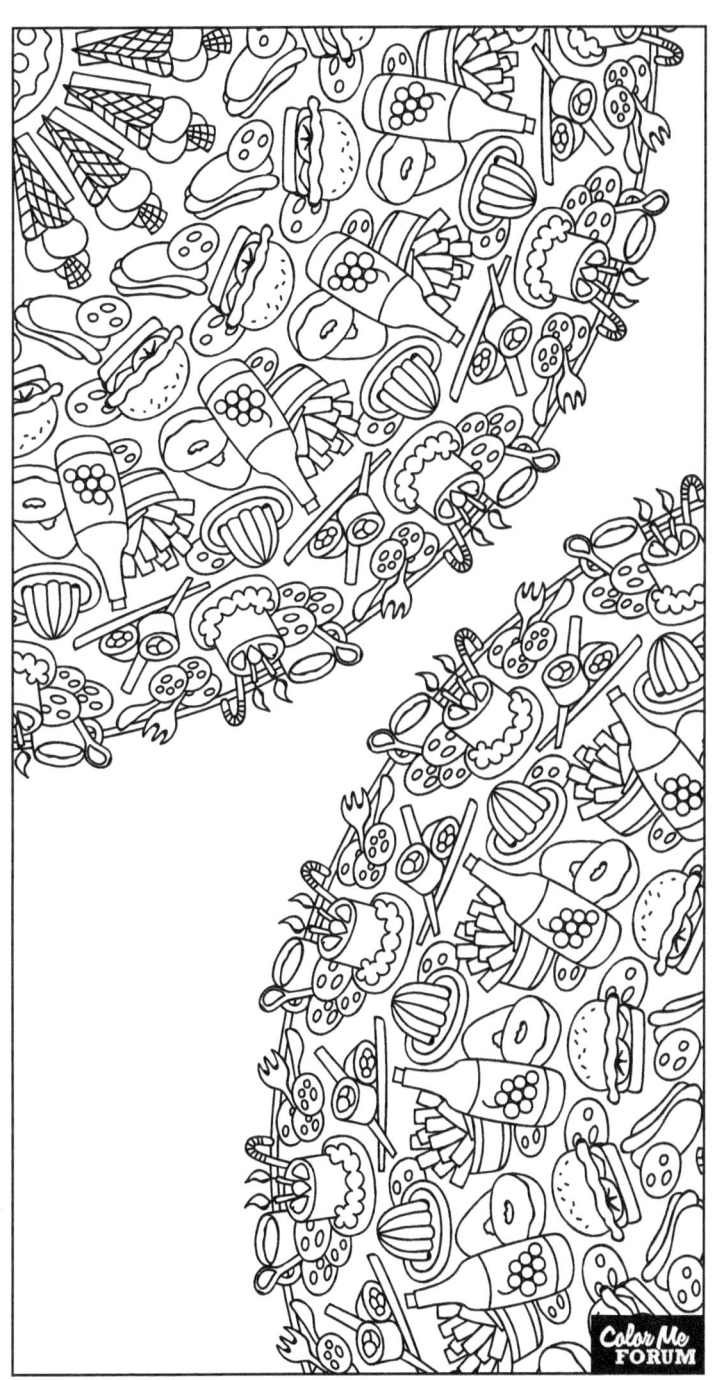

Mandala Teasers by Color Me Forum™

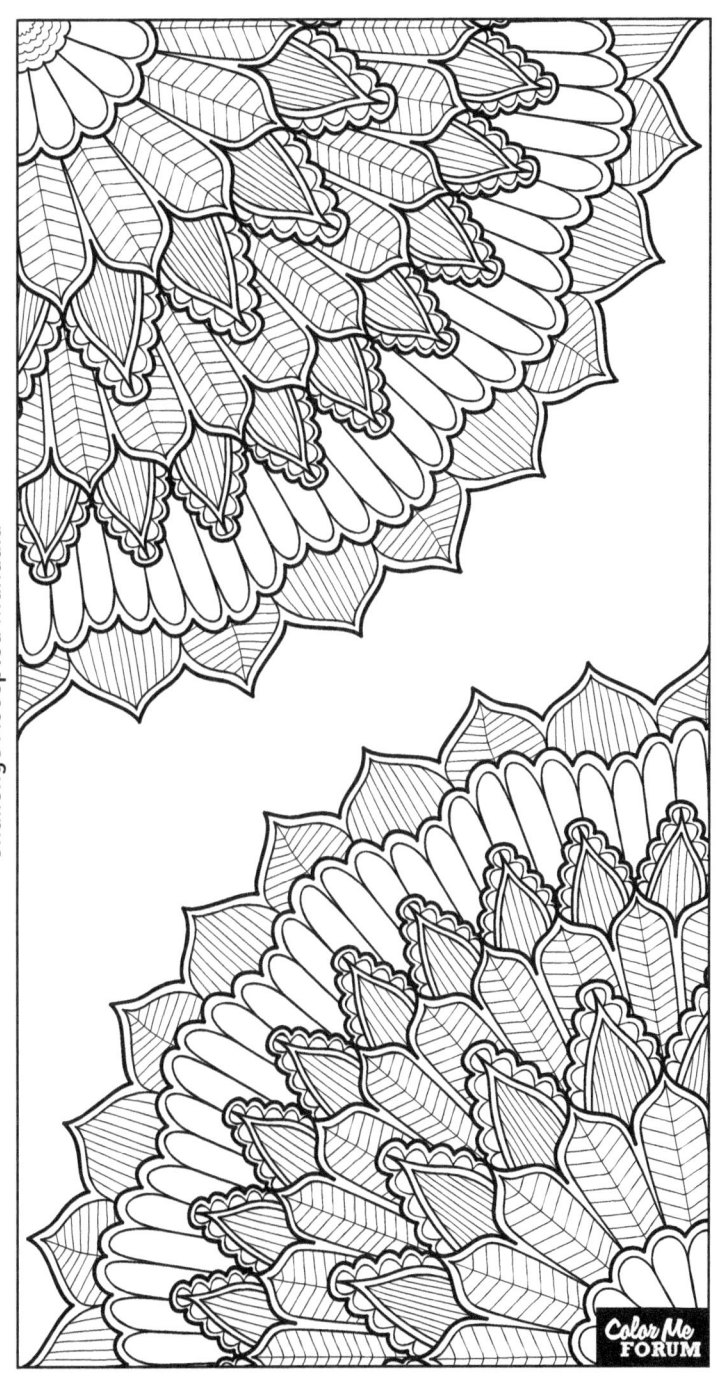

Love Madness Mandala

Mandala Teasers by Color Me Forum™

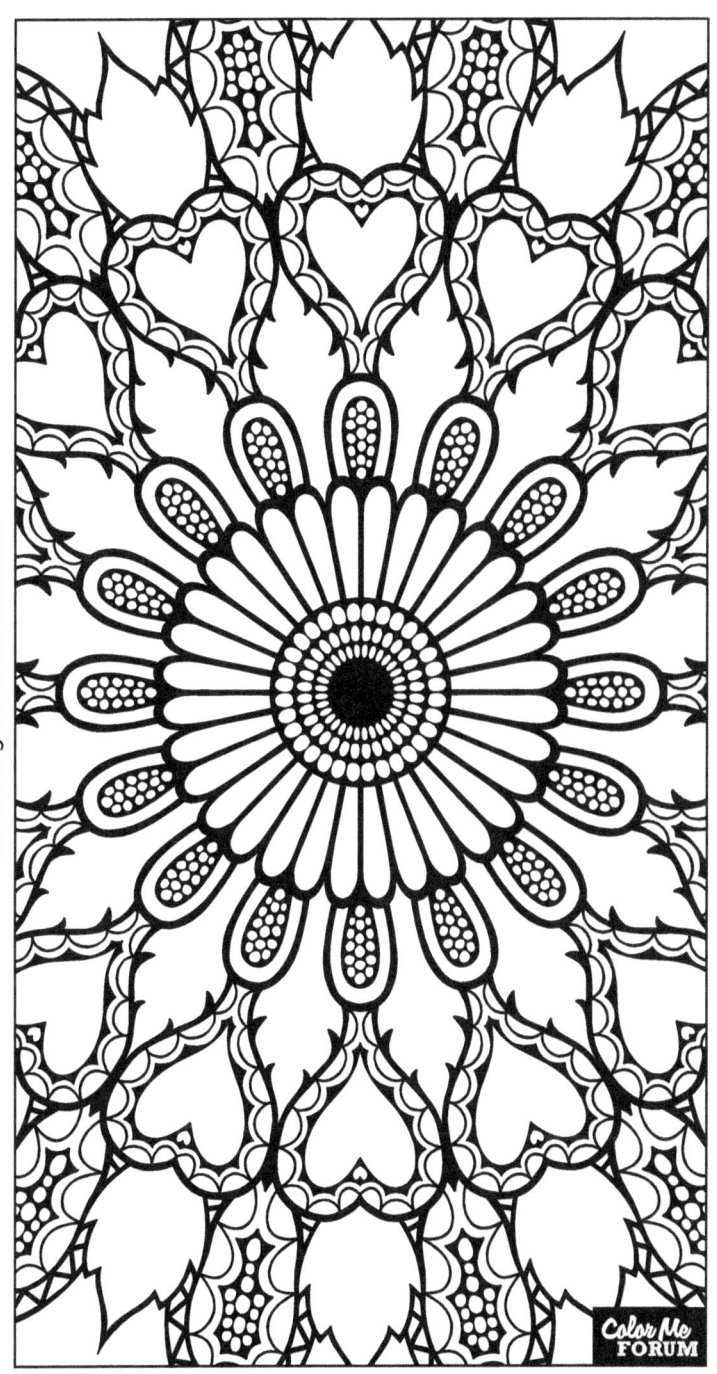

Hearty Flowers Mandala

Mandala Teasers by Color Me Forum™

# Thanks for coloring Mandala Teasers!

These mandala teasers are just teasers for the real thing! If you loved coloring any one of these you can purchase the full sized version from the Color Me Forum store, at **www.ColorMeForum.com/store**.

***As a thank you for purchasing this book you're entitled to 50% off all the full sized versions found inside this book!***

*Simply sign the following page in pen and send a photo to Color Me Forum on Facebook as a private message to get your special coupon!*

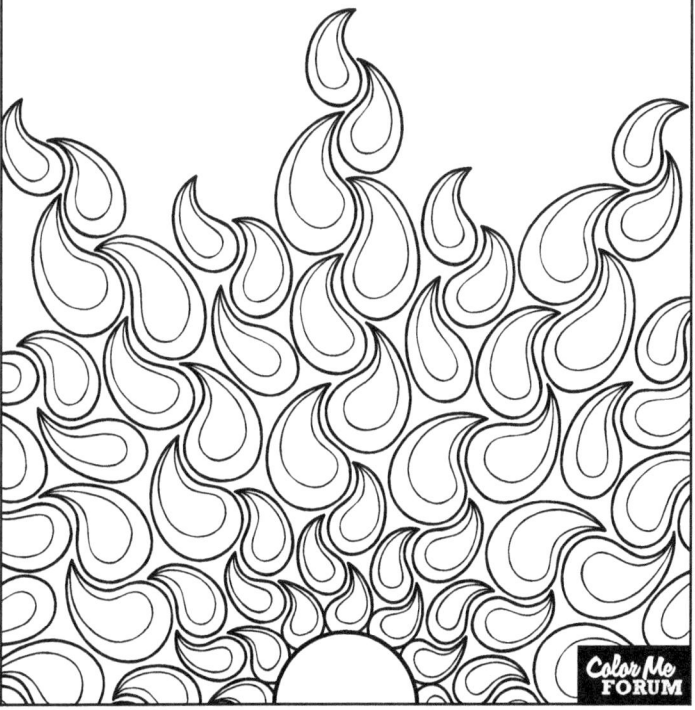

# Redeem Your Coupon!

**Your Name:**

**Your Email (Coupon will be locked to this address):**

**Order Number (If purchased as a PDF ONLY):**

**Your favourite mandala from this book:**

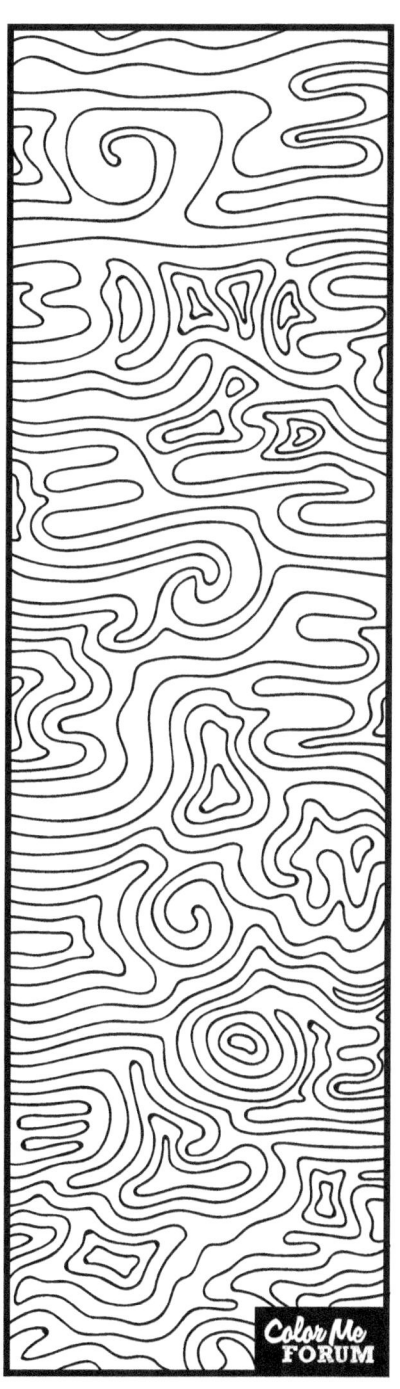

www.ingramcontent.com/pod-product-compliance
Lightning Source LLC
Chambersburg PA
CBHW050017230526
45470CB00003B/1002